A RED
KNOCK-
KNOCKING
LIKE A HEART

LOUISIANA STATE UNIVERSITY PRESS
BATON ROUGE

A RED KNOCK-KNOCKING LIKE A HEART

poems

KATE GASKIN

Published by Louisiana State University Press
lsupress.org

Copyright © 2026 by Kate Gaskin
All rights reserved. Except in the case of brief quotations used in articles or reviews, no part of this publication may be reproduced or transmitted in any format or by any means without written permission of Louisiana State University Press.

LSU Press Paperback Original

DESIGNER: Michelle A. Neustrom
TYPEFACES: Whitman, text; Noah, display

Cover photograph courtesy LaReesa Foy.

Cataloging-in-Publication Data are available from the Library of Congress.

ISBN 978-0-8071-8614-5 (paperback) — ISBN 978-0-8071-8700-5 (pdf) — ISBN 978-0-8071-8701-2 (epub)

For Dax and River
and for the one who almost was

CONTENTS

In Jezero Crater   1

▸ ▸ ▸

Snowscape with ADOS-2   5
Seascape with Palilalia   9
Diagnosis in Reverse   10
Still Life with Mixing Bowl   11
What He's More Than   12
The Field Mice   13
Domestic Taxonomy   14
After the Diagnosis   16

▸ ▸ ▸

Self-Portrait with IUD Failure   19
21 Weeks   20
Landscape with Preterm Labor   22
Authorization for Disposition of Infant Remains   23
After the Baby Dies   24
A Theory of Grief   25
A Theory of Pain   26
Landscape with Mixed Flowers   27
Still Life on the Wrong Side of Statistics   29
The IUD   31
A Theory of Pain   33
21 Weeks   34

▰ ▰ ▰

Domestic Taxonomy   37
Snapshot with Child and Ocean   38
Lightning Dragons   40
Seascape with Ghost Crabs and a Nebula   42
Landscape with Tallgrass and Scales   43
The Owl   45
Mixed Media with Milkweed and an Argument   46
Mountainscape with Mule Deer and Cottonwoods   48
Pastoral with Pink Horses   49
365 Days   51
A Theory of Grief   52
Multiverse with Boybands and Roses   54

▰ ▰ ▰

A Theory of Grief   59
How to Become Alive Again   60
Waiting for Water   61
Rupture   62
Was There Evidence of Malpractice?   64
Sex   66
Cityscape Beginning with a Phrase from *Cosmos*   68
Domestic Taxonomy   69
Marriage as *Ranitomeya imitator*   70
Things I Have Forgotten   72
Landscape with a Possible Unidentified Flying Object   74

Notes and Acknowledgments   77

A RED
KNOCK-
KNOCKING
LIKE A HEART

In Jezero Crater

Whatever was there has gone
        to three and a half billion years
                of dust. On Mars

a rover picks up a rock
        and turns it over
                in a river delta webbed

with dried arteries cauterized
        by the sun. Daughter,
                who lived for only an hour,

I too search for you
        in the most barren places,
                a vein that rolls before

a needle, a dawn that breaks
        dim and drawn. I wish for you
                an emerald canopy,

sapphire water, a world
        where belief is a fact
                that can be held

in my palm like a stone.
        Here on Earth, you disappear
                star-ash, sun-soot, moon-glow

while somewhere above
        in the red star of another planet,
                a robot measures

ancient silt into a vial
        for human hands to touch
                with wonder. What do I do now

                with all this love?

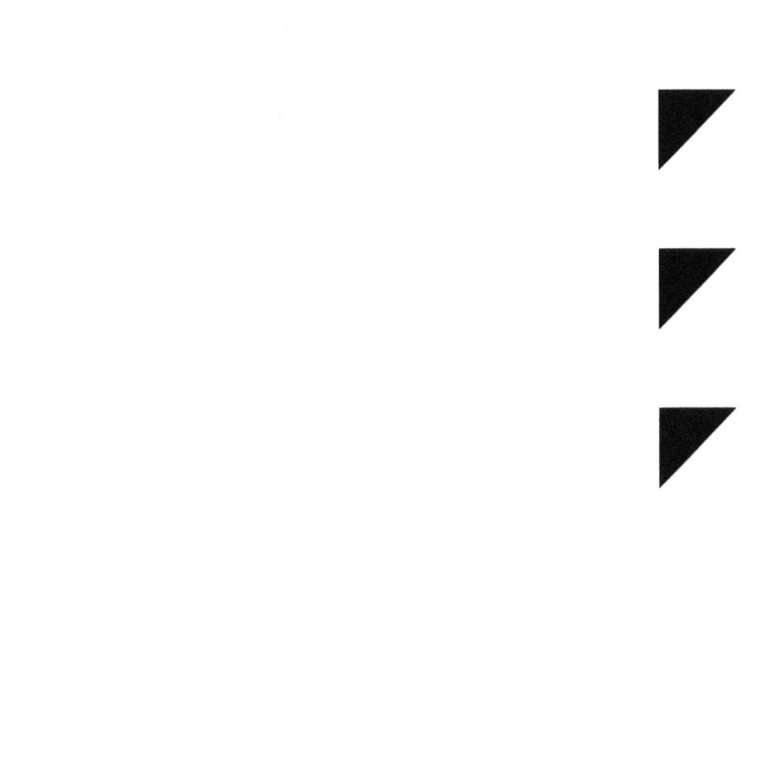

Snowscape with ADOS-2

That was the winter of two snowfalls—flat stretches
of dry roadside sedge hard with frost, and then

a slow accumulation of snow falling
on the steaming streets of Montgomery, Alabama

into potholes, over the roof of the corner store,
its meat-and-three buffet wafting fried chicken

and okra with every warm, humid swing
of the door opening into a frigid December noon.

I had been gone a while, had lived in another flat
city on the edge of a patchwork of prairie

under a July sky, bluest over never-ending
rows of corn. But what I meant to say about snow

in Alabama is that it came twice that winter,
unusual, heavy and wet, weighting the camelias

until they bowed to the ground, their thin stalks
like broken necks. That was my winter of crying

each day on the short trip to my son's kindergarten,
past rows of bougainvillea planted so close to the road

their green fronds brushed the sides of the car
I had to pry him from after I parked behind the school.

That year we took him to a succession
of medical offices, each one beiger than the last,

for test after test, while doctors with blank faces
offered shrugging shoulders and stimulants

and antipsychotics that made him better and then
suddenly worse. Once, he bit me so hard

I slapped him. This isn't about every time
my son kicked me in the shins, or how

once I had to drag him from a children's
museum back to the car where he hit me for half

an hour. Understand, this is a child who could barely
talk, who walked around bleeding and rarely noticed,

who ran from us as soon and as fast as he could
for the sheer joy of running. If I close my eyes

I can see him in his snowsuit, pulling his sled, the year
we moved back to Omaha, my husband helping him

build a snow fort so big that, beside it, he seemed
a tiny red dot in a vast field of white. I'm taking you

forward in time now. I'm showing you he probably
gets better. But first he got worse, my mother

a social worker—thirty-five years—for the poorest county
in Alabama, sitting at our kitchen table in Montgomery

saying, *he's the kind of child I removed from homes,
he's the kind of child people abuse*, a bright blur

of Vyvanse chewables, drops of Dyanavel, Risperdal.
But the snow! Two times it snowed that winter

as I staggered to my neighborhood one-screen
movie theater to sit in the dark and cry

while beautiful men kissed in a sunny Italian villa
or a former Lakota-Sioux rodeo star cared for

his autistic sister in the Badlands of South Dakota.
On my walk home, snow burdened

branches of sweet olive, their deep glossy green
buckling beneath a heavy crust that by morning

was hard and sparkling. Snow was not rare
in Alabama, but it was novel enough

that when thirteen inches fell in 1993 everyone called it
The Great Blizzard. We didn't have power

for a week. I was barely older than my son,
falling and falling in snow that soaked my jeans

as I rolled the body of a snowman and then finished it
with charcoal briquette eyes, a carrot nose,

my grandfather's black fedora. I kept
the photo my mother took on my bedside table, kissing it

each night, promising myself as soon as I could
I would leave for good. Even at ten I wanted

less heat, fewer scrub pines, more snow, city lights
glinting in an icy North I could only imagine

back when I was sure a new place, a new life
would fix me. It snowed twice that Alabama winter.

In the summer I taught him how to pull stamens
clear from honeysuckle blossoms, touch the drops

of nectar to his tongue. What does it mean
to get better? Now, in our yard, he falls backward

into a snowdrift, makes an angel. Listen—
there are church bells in the distance. A pair

of chickadees tut-tut back and forth
across holly cupping small pillows of snow.

Seascape with Palilalia

Is he driven as if by a motor *a motor*
        is he a little red boat

that zips and zooms and does he fall often
        is he often distressed

and does he hit anyone *does he hit* is he
        often distressed or has he ever bitten

does he bite is he a little red boat
        that bobs *bobs* are there calls

calls every day from his teacher
        and which systems run as they should

and should systems fail which ones
        fail first his little socks a limp rainstorm

of socks wet eddies of them in his room
        and through them he boats *he boats*

his boat a little red boat that sinks
        the synapses that sink the structural

abnormalities that sink less gray matter
        less gray matter and reduced cortical

thickness and does he hit the doctor
        does he hit the nurse does he hit

his mother and is he bright *is he bright*
        does he suture the night shut with lightning?

Diagnosis in Reverse

First, the witch turning from the door
made of spiced cake

and sugared almonds. Then the birds
offering the bread back

to the forest floor, the children
skipping backward into the gaunt

yawn of the house as the mother's
long hunger begins

to soften, her hearth dark with smoke.
And then a spark,

the children in the back orchard
eating apricots heavy

with juice. Pale cream in a bowl. A vase
of primroses. Foxglove stirring

outside the open window. The father
coming up the summer path, easy

with evening. Hansel humming.
Fresh bread and long light, long light.

Still Life with Mixing Bowl

My therapist tells me it's not about fixing him,
so when he asks me to make banana bread,
I put aside the old persistent fear that he will
not be okay, that he will be taken—by death
or drugs or jail—and open the cookbook
growing brittle at the spine, its pages yellowing
and marked with splatters of old meals, then
hand him the measuring spoons. Over the book
we bend, as if in prayer, which baking is
of a kind—that bread will rise, that the center
will set, that the boy will measure flour, sugar,
a thimbleful of salt, that this ordinary act
with his mother will be enough, in this moment,
to calm the hurt animal of his nervous system,
to ease his frustration when language is a carrot
and stick. Once, when he was six, I entered
an empty classroom, breathless, to see him
prostrate and screaming, two teachers straining
to hold him down. My therapist says it's about
support, so we bake. We make something good
out of pantry staples and fruit too bruised to eat.

What He's More Than

A flock of common symptoms rising from avoidant
waters, two feet that constantly stumble, an awkward
and irregular gait, a robot in the shape of a boy in the shape
of a dog bounding over a lupine-studded field, a dark
forest patched with spiderwebs and broken-down, archaic
computer parts, limited fixations, a cat sprinting to feel
the wind's sweet breath, a lamp's incandescence, a trampoline's

slingshot propulsion, a loss of speech, a flat affect, a sudden
burst of starlings from a chokecherry tree, a spinning
top, a spinning wheel, yarn unraveling from a favorite
sweater, toy cars arranged in a mile-long queue, a tendency
toward self-harm, a tendency toward tenderness, a tendency
toward tight tendons and tiptoeing feet, a ship washing back
and forth on the sea, a child holding a light in the dark.

The Field Mice

For a week the cat crouched, sentinel
at the kitchen vent. She stalked

the basement floor. We found
her pawprints, the soft wet body

of a mouse, matted fur, bright slash
of flesh. The exterminator promised

a certain quickness. *They really just
dry up. You might find*

a bit of fur or bone. We knew
the poison had worked when the cat

returned to bed at night, yawning,
spinning her lazy circle to cozy

a nest for sleep. All night
something dragged its small body

in the attic above our heads.

Domestic Taxonomy

Everywhere we went, the animals came
as if called: barred owls from tulip trees,
foxes from a tangle of wisteria,
mule deer from among the spun sugar

of cottonwoods, their tassels of winged
seeds billowing white like late snow.
When we lived in Florida, even the dolphins
came to see what we could do. This too

was an omen. And the gray calf, exact
miniature looped to his mother's side,
was portent to our own child, his felted
forehead, marble-round belly, damp eyes

black as interstellar space. How to explain,
then, that we also found them dying
and dead: blue button jellies the color of sea
lying tangled in hundreds along the white

sand beach. A dog shriveled in the summer heat
to a bag of wet leather and tufts of still-
brown fur, its jawbone bright as a pearl.
And the birds. First, the northern flicker

lying next to the front stoop, frozen
in a perfect shock of red and yellow
plumage, its handsome chest spotted
with cream. And next, the fledgling our son

found fallen from the tree. He scooped it
into a box so tenderly, though nothing
can bring back a bird with a snapped neck.
I didn't tell him, then, what's lost often stays

lost, though it was past time to fess up
about moths and their summer dives
into streetlights, or the cat that carried the bird
from the box in a grip that was also love.

After the Diagnosis

Always I am this sorry

body swelling at the least hint of hurt,
childhood like a rag tied up from jaw to temple.
Don't we

ever get to leave anything behind? My sorry

face is your face, my weak
genetic map is your fate. Now you'll never
have your keys when you need them. Your

instinct will be both fight and flight.

Just listen. Just listen. Just listen. We can't be what we
know we are deep down,
less-than and glitchy, cursing our overripe

melons for brains. My son, this is you

now, you always, frenetic blur
of moth wings against bare bulbs, your relentless
porpoising through this, our sea-green world of both

querulous and joyous astonishments. Your anger is my

rage, and your delight incandesces the mean
stinging nettle of my heart. If we are truly in this
together, then we'll always be a little

unlaced, undone, unmoored, unmoved, unimpressed by the

vast difference between
what we know we should do and what we really want, which is
X when X is actually Y when

Y is your whole life unrolling like a carpet of fragrant
zinnias before you, blood-red and flaming and true.

Self-Portrait with IUD Failure

What you snuck past: a vast
copper body, two plastic hands
all the better to twist you from
this empty palace. You are not yet

who you will be, little sac
of yolk, blood clot drifting through.
What should we do with you
who bedded down in a field

of red clover? You want
a piece of cake, meat silky
and tender, slipping free
from the bone. You want my voice

echoing into your chamber.
At night, deer come grazing
into the pasture, and stars unpin
their white-hot hair

with bright fingers orbited
in planetary rings. Congratulations,
you nymph, you nubbin,
you astral tsar. I did not pick you

yet here you are, as in the stray
we plucked from the street,
flea-ridden and matted, lapping
milk from a porcelain bowl.

21 Weeks

In movies, there are always flowers
in the hospital room, but mine was bare.
I had been there four days and was just
beginning to hope I could keep her.

In the hospital room, I was cold and bare
and still bleeding big crimson clots,
though I was beginning to hope I could keep her.
By then I wanted something other than

to be bleeding big crimson clots
so red they were almost purple,
and by then I also wanted something other than
hospital food, so my husband ordered beef ragout

so red it was almost purple
from a restaurant nearby. It was better
than hospital food, this beef ragout
with a salad of microgreens and Peppadews

from a restaurant nearby. It was better
though I picked at it, sitting on my bed
holding a salad of microgreens and Peppadews,
with an IV taped to my hand

as I picked at it, sitting on my bed.
In the morning, the doctors told me to go home
and removed the IV from my hand.
I was stable, they said, no longer in danger

that morning, so they told me to go home.
But there is someone in danger, I said,
though I was stable and no longer in danger
of dying. *But someone here could still die*, I said.

There is someone in danger, I said,
but they sent me home. It was too early to save her
from dying. *But someone here could still die,* I said,
though I was not yet two patients; I was one,

so they sent me home. It was too early to save her,
so I climbed the steps to my bedroom. I wasn't
two patients yet. I was just one.
I knew I couldn't do anything to save her

as I climbed the steps to my bedroom. I wasn't
aware that was the last day I would be with her.
I knew I couldn't do anything to save her.
Afterward, I was alone without her,

and I was aware that was the last day
I would ever be with her.
Afterward, I was alone without her,
and by then there were plenty of flowers.

Landscape with Preterm Labor

      I thought my body
a thick, hardy thing, a big-
horn sheep perched on a jagged
             rock, an elk

fording a snowmelt river,
a fat rattlesnake sunning
      on a dusty boulder.
Today, you are no days older

     than you will ever be,
         little baby,
who never took a breath,
but whose hummingbird

            of a heart
    fluttered for an hour
in the half-light of dawn
        while I held you
    as if in the middle

    of a warm placid lake,
     morning fog rising like
breath from water. New sun.
Old love. First radiance

          of light.

Authorization for Disposition of Infant Remains

My memory sees her as faceless,
the woman who came with forms
into the sunny room

as far away from Labor and Delivery
as possible

in the hospital built
of mirrors and glass and white, white

walls in the newest part of town.
Outside, yellow coneflowers and wild parsnip
bloomed by the strip mall

across the interstate
where I'd bought elastic-waist pants
and roomy cotton dresses

just weeks before.
Even in Paris where we never were
I wait for you,

I must have said. To the woman
I must have said, *Yes, yes,*

that one, and picked the funeral home
from a list printed on paper,
while eating a cheese omelet

and stripping orange slices
from their rind with my teeth.

After the Baby Dies

Neil brings over a lasagna,
says he'll do anything

to help. It's spring. Blustery.
He has a new black lab,

a puppy named Bella
who barks at me

through Neil's new fence.
Neil was a nurse

in a maternity ward
for many years and knows

what I now know,
that sometimes babies slip

past the sheer silk
of their lives into a final dusk.

Sitting in my backyard,
I watch Neil train Bella

to *sit, now stand, now fetch
this stick*. What a good girl

she is. Paws up,
and now they're dancing.

It's warm. My arms
are empty. The sun is bright.

A Theory of Grief

At afterschool pickup
outside the entrance

to my son's school,
none of the mothers would look at me. They formed

a wall with their darting, rabbity
glances. Trees budded white as spittle

above us. I am asking you
to be kinder,

or I am asking them to forgive themselves for not knowing
how. Dusk threw its velvet curtains

against the fragile light. At night, the tulips
were tight as fists.

A Theory of Pain

That spring, I moved
wincingly, as if an animal

too difficult to look at

closely, a rabbit limping,
trailing a bleeding paw,
or a dog you pass

on the side of the road,
thinking, *No*—and then, worse,
you see her

raise her head from the asphalt,
and it's too much

to look at, looking leading

to actually seeing
the black fur, the soft
brown muzzle, wet eyes,

the helplessness that lies
at the center, which we drink

or fuck or spend away
to avoid feeling

how we feel, seeing her
on the gray road at the very beginning
of the gray spring, the trees beginning

to wake up,
to swell obscenely in the sky.

Landscape with Mixed Flowers

After she died
the crocuses bloomed

and the purple phlox.
The daffodils bloomed

and the snowdrops.
The star magnolias bloomed

and the forsythia.
The crabapples bloomed

and the redbuds.
The jewelweed bloomed

and the wild stonecrop.
The rue anemone bloomed

and the oxeye daisy.
The bindweed bloomed

and the blue-eyed grass.
The grape hyacinth bloomed

and the chickweed.
The purple deadnettle bloomed

and the tickseed and the bloodroot,
and the spring air

was thawed ice
and crushed petals and powdered sex,

and I walked through it slantly,
stutteringly, as if driven forth by

a nightmare, seeing everything
through the new prism

of the sudden and horrible
dream logic of my life.

Still Life on the Wrong Side of Statistics

Eight years, thin copper, penny-bright.

And hidden in deep red. Once, a doctor told me.

He couldn't see the strings. I, a good girl.

All these years and perfect birth control.

The ultrasound showed it tucked in its gray box.

Little white T. I never didn't practice.

Sex like a textbook description of.

I was that safe. The product pamphlet says.

Ten years, and on the eighth. Is it an urban legend?

The one about the baby born clutching an IUD?

In its chubby hand? Statistically, it was less.

Than a 1 percent chance, what happened.

To me. When she began. A baby.

And I, so careful. So responsible. The doctors said.

It probably wasn't the IUD that caused it.

The doctors said it was probably the IUD.

That caused the labor before she could.

Before she was. Afterward, it was like.

I didn't have her. Though I had had her, she was never.

She was two pieces of paper. Eventually, it fell.

Into the toilet: swift bloom of blood, copper wire.

The IUD

It was ironclad, and it also failed,
      which was the genesis
           of the hurt that visited afterward

          monstrous as an angel beating down
     from above. I want to say something
about darkness, how biblical it was

to carry a seed I didn't want.
      For weeks I kept a card in my purse
          with the number of a clinic

         that could change my life back.
    What happened next
isn't about being punished

though I am sure of cosmic backlash
     to my pettiness, my small-mindedness,
         how I never want to be the one

         to stop on the side of the road and help.
     The baby died. I watched her, held her
as she did. It wasn't karma.

It was like a reverse visitation, giving up
     something I had never been meant
        to keep. Is it cruel

        to spend a whole life like this—
    wanting and not wanting and wanting,
waffling wildly among love

and desire and doubt,
> like a pack of cards being shuffled
>> and reshuffled, landing always

>>> and only on the heart?

A Theory of Pain

We were at a long table, candles flickering in the breeze,
outside on the deck that overlooks the bay, which was black

and tinseled where moonlight fell on the wrinkled silk
of reflected stars shivering with the water, and my brother
was asking my sister if she was still seeing the same doctor

for this newest baby, four months in utero, a celebrated baby
who had come a year after an early miscarriage, and I was

listening, drinking a bottle of cold beer and watching
the candleflames move with the wind as it blew in from
the ocean and skipped in ripples across the blackwater bay,

and my baby was three months dead; she was in a tiny urn
in my bedroom while my brother flicked a lighter on, off, on,

off, and my sister said, yes, she was still seeing the same
doctor, and I was at the table with candles and dessert plates,
empty now, that had held thin slices of cold key lime pie; I was

sitting there among my candlelit family, surrounded by rows
of empty glass bottles, a breeze whistling across their tops.

21 Weeks

A death not quite

a death, but all the same
for five months you were

amphibian, amniotic

a heart bobbing
in rhythm with mine.

Outside, so many starlings

perch on an oak branch
it sways beneath them

hundred-eyed and winged.

In the hospital, I said
This is it and got down

to the work of bearing you

though you could not yet
bear the air. Daughter

a brief of pelicans skims low

across the bay tonight.
It is the labor

of my life to love you.

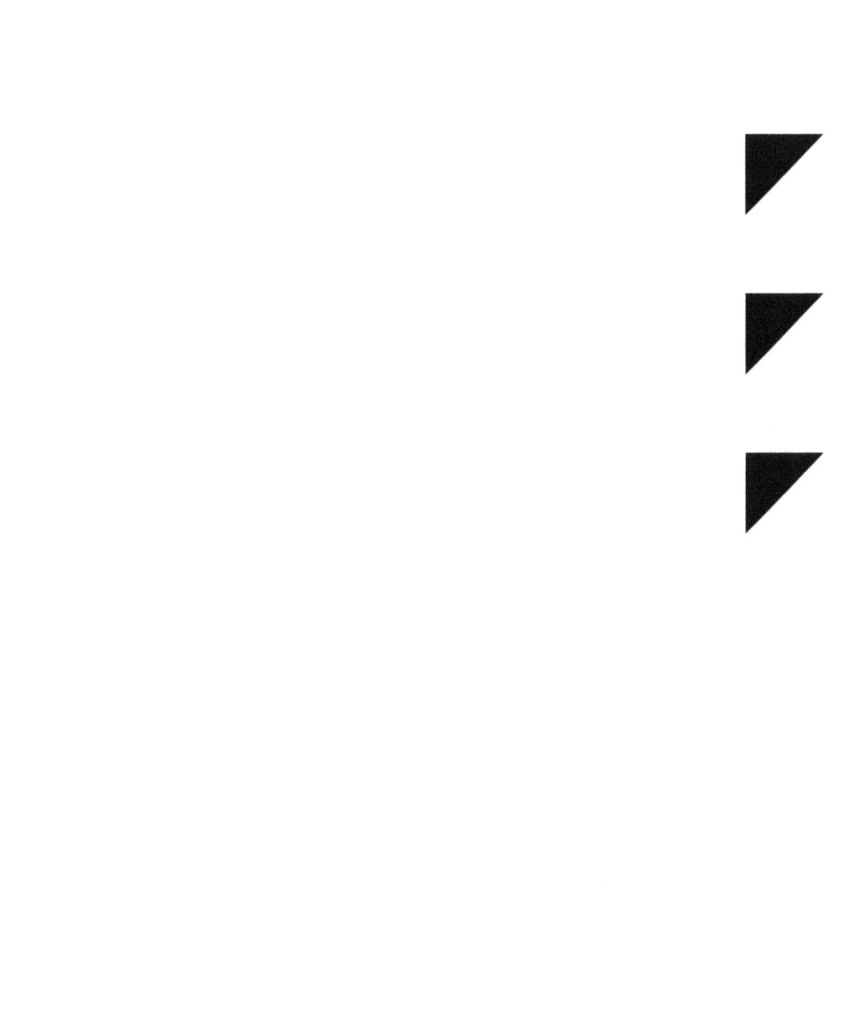

Domestic Taxonomy

Often, they came with the tide and stayed
        for days—moon jellies, pink meanies,

Portuguese man o' wars snagging the breeze
        with their puffed and iridescent sails.

We walked onto the dock and counted
        handfuls, tentacles drifting behind them

like spectral rags. But on purple flag days,
        when they clotted the bay,

we knew to stay out of the water.
        Most afternoons, we put our son down

for his nap and then walked outside to see
        what we could find: blue crabs and stingrays,

fat redfish cooling in the shade, a snatch
        of silver mullet in our neighbor's net, and, yes,

sometimes there were nothing but jellyfish,
        so thick they coagulated the sea,

back when we loved so much we loved
        it all, even the venomous things.

Snapshot with Child and Ocean

He emerges slick as a fish
from the surf, still in his clothes, jeans

hanging off his slim hips like a scarf
slipping from a hook. His smile

is made more of shock from cold
than delight as he runs up the beach

and falls backward, making,
yes, a sand angel. It's Christmas,

and here, among skittering sandpipers
and clams with one foot digging down,

there is, for a moment, relief
from days on end of dysfunction,

how once he slapped me
so hard my glasses flew off and broke.

I don't assign fault. I assign hope
to my panicked heart even

in dead winter, bare trees, and years
of illness and dysregulation,

the way they moved into our house,
inconsolable as a haunting, a ghoul

squatting at the foot of our stairs.
Here, at least, there's sun, so much

you squint and still can't see
every joyful thing, the box turtle

he helped cross the street
and released into saw palmettos that turn

to scrub pine and dune lavender
cascading into the sea. I can't promise

anything, that winter will break
or spring will haul itself up, hand

over hand, from root to bud. Likely,
there will be thaw. We know this

from history. Likely, he'll stand up
sandy and laughing. We'll eat

cheeseburgers on the way home,
read a story, go to bed. A woodpecker

will wake us in the morning,
a red knock-knocking like a heart.

Lightning Dragons

It's a terrible thing to say,
  but imagining my son's death
    comes as naturally to me

as watching a cat trot off
  with a bird clenched in its jaws.
    Today, there is a crushed

cedar waxwing in the street,
  its golden tail feathers splayed,
    the red cherry of its chest

popped open like a mouth.
  I found it on my run and thought
    how impossible it is

to be so small, so easily undone.
  This boy of mine runs
    away from me into busy streets.

A museum's noisy crowd
  swallows him whole. At school
    he cannot sit still or listen.

Once, his teacher said he threatened
  another child with the sharp end
    of a pencil. I did not

believe her, but what I believe
  will not keep him safe
    from how others

inevitably perceive him,
  and so I imagine
    what it would be like to lose him

as he tells me about dragons,
        how there are four types:
                sun dragons, moon dragons,

rain dragons, and, his favorite,
        lightning dragons that hatch
                from eggs that erupt

in shocks of electromagnetic
        radiation. See them flying now?
                He points to the night sky,

its feathery moon and stars
        like puncture wounds, while above us
                heat lightning unsettles

                the dark.

Seascape with Ghost Crabs and a Nebula

I don't mean to imply a history
of constant dysfunction. There was a stretch

of bay out back, blue as cornflowers,
and blooms of moon jellyfish pulsing over

baby stingrays in the sand. One year I ran
down a road thick with orange trees

and star jasmine to a park that ended
in sea, past dunes golden with oats

and ghost crabs poking in and out
of hidden dens. My child was happy then,

and even in the years since,
on days when our home has been nothing

but a low moan, we've been happy,
though once my husband kicked

the wall, and once my son kicked
my legs and ran into a busy street

without looking. One night I heard screaming
and realized it was me. One night

we watched football, ate chicken wings,
licked the bones clean, then tucked him

into bed, snug in X-Wing sheets.
A lamp rolled a pink galaxy

onto his ceiling, bright and hopeful
as a nebula in the darkest palm of space.

Landscape with Tallgrass and Scales

At the end of summer, my son
brings me a snakeskin, pale paper
pocked in tidy rows. He holds

this parchment-brittle wisp
with pride. I know it's a garter
because that's the only snake

I've seen in the groomed hostas
of this tamed prairie. In *My Ántonia*
rattlesnakes once parted junegrass

and bluestem as if small gods,
and in legions, so plentiful they were,
well fed on rabbit and vole,

even the occasional heel of a child
running by, bonnet in hand.
But today, in land cleared

and drained for corn and alfalfa,
Cather's rattlesnakes are mostly gone,
though once a friend told me

a story about her family's ranch
in South Dakota, the pack of cousins
she ran with, tight and lean as coyotes

trotting through switchgrass,
until a sudden movement, a sting.
The cousins' frantic yelling

summoned her parents who threw her
into the family station wagon.
Only one fang had struck

the back of her calf—half
the venom—and so she lived. My kid
once spotted a copperhead coiled

in the woods of Alabama, but here
in midtown Omaha, among neat
sidewalks and heavy-headed peonies,

all we have are garter snakes
ribboning through groundcover,
shedding into tender, slightly bigger

versions of themselves, their old lives
catching like sheer tissue on a bit
of dry root hooking out

from a lawn-green hill
for a lonely little boy,
who cannot control his vastness

of feeling, to find as treasure—
a sheer map, a wild thing
slipped free, intact, in one perfect sleeve.

The Owl

It flew so close overhead—wingtip to wingtip
as large as a child—that, startled, my first impulse
was to reach out and graze its mottled feathers:
this plainly wild thing, suddenly strange
among the neighborhood's groomed camellias
and shiny black sedans parked under powerlines
sagging with wisteria. Soon after, I saw its mate

in the hickory tree behind our back shed.
A family, then. This was the year of illness,
the year I cried as moonlight ran shadows
up my bedroom wall, and then again when I woke
to the same bright sun while the pair of them
settled into their trees for the day, the way sorrow
roosts so quietly you don't see it until it's there.

Mixed Media with Milkweed and an Argument

All day we were at it, not
bickering but cold, cordial, the way

you can punish without punishing,
thrush-tongued and bitter seed

of so much left unsaid, clamp-
mouthed as oysters. I remember

the time we lived by the sea.
Your parents watched our son

as we drank cold beer in the fog
while the barges rolled in,

and, later, when the monarchs
flocked south in thick orange swells,

if we stood still long enough
they stopped to drowse in our hair

as if we were tufts of milkweed,
though we could give them

nothing sweet. Those were the nights
we loved each other best.

By which I mean easily, the curtains
blowsing in, the ospreys fat

with fish, spitting bones onto the dock
through shrills of mating frogs. And now

this night, its pinched mouth
and sterile air, your shoulders not far

from where I lie burning to touch
you, even now, after all these years.

Mountainscape with Mule Deer and Cottonwoods

There were never children.
There was only a herd

of mule deer, ragged at the ears,
grazing in the soft pasture

and then nesting beside the gravel path
we walked daily, holding hands.

There were mountains.
There were thistles,

their throats thorned with purple needles.
There was even a snake swallowing

a baby rabbit, but there were never
children, never daily illness

or sorrow strung limp from the trees
like wet sheets. There were only deer

lying beside cottonwoods
bailing out armfuls of white wooly seeds

so that even in June there was snow.

Pastoral with Pink Horses

It was deep summer. The grasses
were all golden. Amber bales
of hay, rolled tight

as cinnamon buns, lay dotted
around a lone field oak, with horses
grazing between. Years later,

after we were married, after the birth
of our son, the death
of our daughter, we went

to see a neighbor's Appaloosas,
thinking they'd be prancing the white
fencing of their pen, a lush rug

of green grass unspooling down
to a cobalt fishpond. Idyllic. But
the horses had less than a quarter-acre

to pace back and forth on land that was worn
of all grass. Anything green was shorn
down to the red clay, so that the horses,

which were spotted fawn and cream,
had stained themselves pink
with their rolling.

We took our son to see them
as therapy. Isn't that what you do
with a clinically unhappy child?

But he was scared, and the flies were bad,
and the farm dog kept lunging at us
with glee that blurred feral.

It wasn't like I'd pictured, our life,
fifteen years after we first went driving
down these country roads together,

windows down, my hair in a cumulus
cloud floating around my face.
Could it get any better, falling in love

in September when even
the air was honey, even the water
was honey? Knowing now what I know

about how things would go—the hospitals
and doctors' offices, the flickering
fluorescent sorrow particular

to rooms where diagnoses and babies
are delivered, how death came
and life too—well, what was there to do

that day except watch pink horses
in their little pen under pines that stretched
all the way, I swear, to something

as awful, as luminous as heaven.

365 Days

During which I should have had you
in July, dewy with heat, milk-full. Then

        fireworks. The tiger lilies' speckled
        orange tongues flickering in the half-

dark yard. You, in a box on my dresser
during a wild September snow, the trees'

        branches snapping in half as easily
        as dandelion stems. One by one, sudden

woundings. Then Halloween, your brother
running down the sidewalk, velvet dusk

        gathering in his hair. Next, Thanksgiving
        and Christmas, and suddenly I am

no longer in the year of your birth, neither
the day predicted, nor the day when you

        arrived, too early, breathless, into a cold
        pink dawn. And then I'm counting down

to March, dreading the day you were born
all over, how the moment you came to be

        in the world plays in my head on a stage
        with a curtain that will not close.

A Theory of Grief

Because dusting is a chore I don't like,
I've left a thin film on every object
under my care for the past thirty years,

tolerating—instead—
the furred, the dusky, the dirty blur
dust makes of brass lighting fixtures,

the fine, particulate layer of gray that settles
on every wooden mantel and bookshelf.
I'm not next to Godliness

when it comes to cleanliness
is what I'm saying.
I could go years without

a single swipe of an old rag or feather duster,
which is why when I clean the blue velvet case
that cushions your vase of ashes,

it is, for a moment, the holiest part
of my day. A lint roller works best.
I hold you and begin to lift

the days, the weeks, the years
from the only skin you have now, stripping
dust from the soft fabric of your cheek,

which is also dust, as I will be one day,
as your father will be too.
Dust, from the mouth of the Big Bang

that ignited this world. Dust, in the wind
that blows from shore to troubled shore.
Dust, falling in glittering motes

onto a sleeping cat.
Dust, which is you,
skimming the soft blue fabric

encasing your only home, which is a vase
of dust. Swipe after gentle swipe,
particle by golden particle,

I lift you. I hold you. I let you go.

Multiverse with Boybands and Roses

Sometimes I like to imagine another life
one in which
the daughter I lost at birth

is thirteen now
and leaning away from me
suddenly into a future

of lip gloss and friends
and chatrooms and did I mention
it's still the 90s there

in this other dimension this other
timeline perforated
at the edge of technology

before it explodes twenty years
from now but for now she is spritzing
body spray she is popping

strawberry gum she has the best news
to tell her best friend
about a boy she met in a chatroom

for people who love boybands
and while they talk they listen
to Sidestreet Boys sing

"Fate of My Heart" on the pink
boombox she got for Christmas
and neither of them

will have flesh and blood
non-pixelated boyfriends for years
but until then there's debate

and dance and music
and her dad's new speedboat
on sunny days wind in her hair

lake spray on her face
and the bracingly cold delight
of bobbing in the deepest parts

of the dammed river while over
on Chimney Rock another boy jumps
from fifty feet and this time

he hits the water just right doesn't sever
his spinal cord doesn't surface
face down and limp

and motionless his friends yelling
at him to stop teasing
no the water is safe today and the boy

grows up to become an orthodontist
who on weekends plays trumpet
in the local jazz band

and now it's the golden hour
of the afternoon and my daughter
is lying on a lounge chair

among the French hydrangeas
and Coral Knock Outs her dad planted
and she is glowing she is bronzed

from head-to-toe painting
her toenails humming a little tune
that doesn't exist in this time

or place but is a big hit
where she lives unbothered by
the accident of her conception

in another timeline
where I—her mother—am staring
with dismay at the test

in my hands and then months later
holding her small still body
a baby who will never be anything

but stardust or atomized matter
glittering in the unreachable
expanse between where I am here

and where she is there
literally breath and blood
and beauty in the bright light

that saturates her dad's garden
listening to a song
that somehow all of us know by heart.

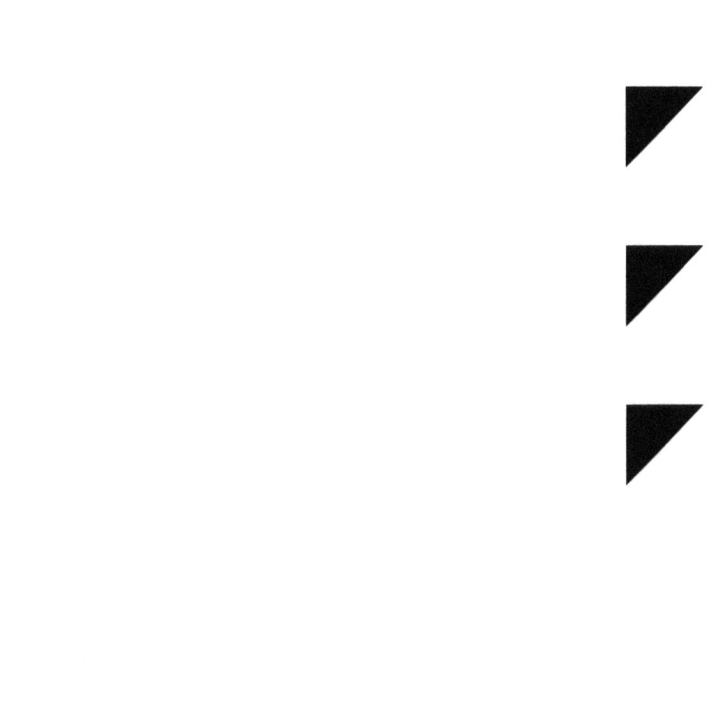

A Theory of Grief

        I didn't think I could be wanted
        again, breasts soft, your head against
                the empty bag of my stomach,
        but blood sounds its ocean

of desire, held to the ear like a conch,
and once I said yes, you bent over me,
            rolling on a condom,
    your hands like my own hands,

love remaking itself, terrible and desperate,
                          out of nothing,
                  out of the crown of her
                  head as we held her

                and then the memory of her,
                      now even smaller,
                  pressed and precious
as amber.

How to Become Alive Again

Buy a leather jacket for your heart.
Sit on the edge of your bed and stare.
Follow your grief into every room
as it leads you on a leash.
Notice when the cottonwoods release
their seeds all at once, the wind frothy
with floating tufts of airy hair.
Go to a party and stay for one hour.
After that hour passes, disappear
from your corporeal being until
you are a warm orb of light wearing
shearling-lined slippers. Pierce
something, probably just your ears
again. Maybe your nose. Wade
into an ocean despite the bull sharks
cruising the lapis lazuli length
of the shore. Poke a stranded jellyfish
with a stick. Fuck your husband.
Fuck your husband. Let a cat make
a nest of your body as you nap
beneath a buttery spindle of light.
Hold a small vase of ashes
in one hand. Hold that hand with
your other hand. Become a body
made just of hands. You feel your
way through the world like this now—
a million milky nerve endings
softened and stretched thin.

Waiting for Water

Suddenly, I understood the gorilla's kitten
given to her after she signed *baby*
and then cried in the spare concrete pad
of her enclosure. I understood, too,
certain women's obsessions with dolls
painted to look like alarmingly real babies,
exact in facial folds of fat, clear blue
eyes, and cupid's bow lips. It's not that I
thought I could replace her, but my body—
so recently busy knitting the bones and skin
and strands of DNA into her perfect,
tiny hands—needed an occupation. Like a cup
sitting on a table, waiting for water.
It was like that. Needing to be used
for that one specific purpose, to quench
a thirst, to be filled all the way up.

Rupture

The surgeon who saved my life
        said my uterus looked

like a tomato that had been squeezed
        into soft pulpy flesh

bursting from split skin
        when my doctor arrived I was

already under
        whiter and clammier

than chicken skin beneath
        cellophane under sharp

fluorescent lights
        with her phone she took

pictures of it lying
        on a shiny surgical tray

like a slab of raw meat
        jagged along the side

where it had ruptured
        later she showed it to me

as I sat on an exam table my legs
        swinging under me like a child's

when I woke all anyone could
        talk about was my color-

less lips my face how I had
        almost disappeared

Where is the baby I said
        over and over Where is he

Like a tomato bursting the surgeon
        said If you'd been anywhere else

at home or even
        at a smaller more rural hospital—

Your color looks better
        my husband said over and over

the baby was intubated
        in an incubator

my husband showed me pictures
        what do they do with leftover body parts

I thought about smokestacks
        the incinerator

where someone had placed
        our daughter the year before

Your color looks better
        he was attached to the wall with wires

there were tubes down his nose
        and throat an IV in his tiny head

but he wasn't I wasn't he wasn't
        I wasn't he wasn't I wasn't dead

Was There Evidence of Malpractice?

A good question, but I'm not sure. Healthcare
being what it is in this country, being

cut from rough cloth. Burlap, say,
dyed scarlet. Statistically, I mean, I was in

error, an anomaly, blood streaking the bright
floor of the OR. A woman can

go where she is told, be good,
have all the right answers and still not be

in possession of her own mind, her own body,
judged competent, trusted. Her

kind, I mean. They kept turning it up,
little drip to make the contractions stronger,

make them more frequent.
No matter that suddenly they were too—too—

Oh, but I had done it before and knew what
possible outcomes to expect. Afterward, I

questioned my doctor. My uterus had
ripped right up the side, she said. She said

she'd never seen anything like it. When
the first, then second, then third nurse turned

up the Pitocin, I knew. Pain
voraciously eating a black hole through the hot

weather of my body. I didn't die though I wanted to.
X-rays showed the baby's heart, his lungs, his kidneys.

You can't force a woman, or you can. Oh, I chose. I
zeroed in on his breath, on his chest moving up and down.

Sex

Surely, after twenty years together, we've had
enough. Enough nights

to line up in a row
and make more than enough miles

to take us from Ambrose Light, New York,
all the way across the Atlantic

to Lizard Point, Cornwall. A whole ocean
of nights! Haven't I been touched

enough? Haven't I met danger over
and over, and by the only man

who I ever felt was safe enough
to love? This is what I asked of you

from the very beginning, to meet me
in that sunlit room and trust

that the thing between us, which sparked
and sputtered and spit,

would spare us both. It's not fair
to say the babies came too easily

because we were so good at it,
but there are days I'm sure my body

was made to pocket yours, like a sock
tucked into another sock, like gloves folded

and locked in a pair. And even when
it scared me, when it hurt,

I knew that between us there was something
old as stone, as magma moving the plates

of the earth, this ancient thing
that men die for, that women die from,

that people roam the whole dark forest
of history to find.

Cityscape Beginning with a Phrase from *Cosmos*

And you are made of a hundred trillion cells
and every one of them is trembling.
You go grocery shopping

for fun, bring back the fancy shortbread cookies
I love. There are hooks and eyes, fallows
and wheat, spans of unbridgeable distance

between now and whatever's coming. *Tell me
you love me*, I say. It's simple. You call me over
to see the red-tailed hawk perched on a lamppost

in our ordinary neighborhood, in the ordinary
street. The day is long and yellow, and despite
our sorrow we're here, standing beneath

its rust-colored feathers, its magnificent wings.

Domestic Taxonomy

The flue was closed, the windows shut,
        the basement sealed. And yet

it appeared in our bedroom, a velvety
        quick flutter of smooth leather, snatch

of dark night, glossy fur, and storybook
        webbed wings. I wanted it out

with everything in my body, unable
        to bear its frantic circles skimming the air

from bed corner to dresser drawer
        to the arch above the window. Name

a revulsion: slithering or buzzing
        or skittering or crawling and then add

wings. Remember the summer when we
        descended the slick wooden stairs

into the cold water of the cave?
        Above us, a whirling constellation of bats.

I want so badly not to fear what I don't know.
        Up close their snouts are canine, their black

eyes unblinkingly sweet and round,
        but in the room where we make love

and I nursed our children, I want nothing feral
        to breach, no need or desire or demand

to break frantically over my head
        like a heart, bright and wildly beating.

Marriage as *Ranitomeya imitator*

In the education room of Wind Creek State Park,
which is really just a windowless equipment shed,

I listen to a park ranger talk about frogs
while I hold our baby on my lap as our older son

feigns death from boredom. *The bullfrog breeds
from March to August,* the ranger says. *Its song*

sounds like a cow. I know this place well,
have biked from lake-end through cool pine woods

and back through a childhood laced
with the smell of grilled burgers and spitting firewood.

The baby sits quietly while our oldest fidgets and groans.
You're away in Las Vegas for work all summer

while I visit my parents in Alabama, and we need
something to do. The ranger shows a picture

of the little grass frog. *No bigger than some mosquitos.
You won't see it unless you look.* I envy

its ability to disappear. At the end of the week
I leave the kids with their grandparents,

board a plane, and fly through purple dusk
all the way to Nevada. We leave bed

only to drive across a city gilded with mirrors and fountains
sparkling against a moonscape of black and white sand.

You point out markers of your childhood.
This is the stadium where I graduated high school.

My friends and I went to Circus Circus when we were bored.
I still want to know everything about you

though I've known you twenty years. Nevada has frogs too,
of course—the Northern leopard frog,

the red-spotted toad, the Great Basin spadefoot.
What is it about our particular kind of love

that lasts? *Frogs aren't monogamous.*
They mate and scram, the ranger says. *Except*

for Peruvian Ranitomeya imitators,
a couple of real stand-up amphibians

who stick around for the kids. Between the two of us
we try, but we keep replicating

our mistakes. My forgetfulness. Your argumentative
streak. *Only one in fifty eggs survives.* For once

I'm not talking about the baby we lost. For once
I'm saying everything's terrible

but okay. This is family: a failure
to love tepidly, to live quietly, to honor

our promise that it was, at any point, ever
possible to keep each other safe.

Things I Have Forgotten

Names, dates, your birthday
though I've spent twenty of them with you.
The way home. How to do
long division. How to swaddle
a baby. Our oldest son at school
stranded by the band room, his sneakers kicking
at loose gravel. Mother's Day
though I am a mother. Father's Day
though I have a father, though I have made
of you a father. I've forgotten girlishness,
who I was before the deep griefs
moved in with their lead suitcases,
settling in and turning off the lamps
in the empty rooms of my chest.
I've forgotten what it's like
to be alone, I who have loved
and been loved
so deliberately, so consistently,
our sons' need for me like a homing missile
trained on the heat of me
as I run down the tedious minutes of my day
driving to work, or making small talk,
or heating my lunch in the microwave.
Forgotten—the wash in the washing machine.
The cat's empty food bowl.
The route to my best friend's childhood house.
Nothing is safe
from the closefisted gelatin
of my hapless brain
capable of so much and yet still
peddling recklessly like a monkey on a bicycle
over the tightrope of my life.
Remember that ordinary day
in April when we stripped the stained wallpaper
from our new bedroom

and I asked about all your old girlfriends?
It must have made you feel young again
thinking of the pretty faces and long legs
I'd only ever seen in stacks of blurry
photographs. What you did to me afterward.
Even in the darkness, in the long hallway
I will eventually walk down alone,
please let me never forget.

Landscape with a Possible Unidentified Flying Object

All this glittering city

and yet we are still only
animals and heat
and the renewable resource

of tears.

Bodies will always make more room
for grief.
There's the known

and unknown: someone will hurt you

by hurting himself, apples
make a healthy snack, a shower is a good
place for crying. And sometimes

in the sky at night there are phenomena

we don't yet know how to name. I'm tired
of running down the same hallway
of my handful of faults,

never learning which doors

lead to which rooms, and—never mind—
they're all locked anyway. I want to live
in the mystery of what I can't describe,

how time loops

us back to our origin stories, each of us
dragging our tin cans of sorrow behind.
Give me a bouquet of unexplained lights

unzipping into the color of cornflowers

above the Gateway Arch. I want to believe
I can go beyond my own understanding
of this plainly heartbroken world—

its starfish, wild fruit, and gleaming.

NOTES & ACKNOWLEDGMENTS

Notes

"Snowscape with ADOS-2" is after John Murillo.

"Authorization for Disposition of Infant Remains" contains lines from Ruth Stone's poem "Turn Your Eyes Away."

"Still Life on the Wrong Side of Statistics" is after Jacques J. Rancourt.

"A Theory of Pain [We were at a long table . . .]" is after Marie Howe.

"Landscape with Tallgrass and Scales" is for LaReesa Foy.

"Marriage as *Ranitomeya imitator*" takes inspiration for its title from Nicole Cooley.

Acknowledgments

Grateful acknowledgment is made to the editors of the following publications, in which the poems listed first appeared, sometimes in slightly different versions or under different titles:

American Poetry Review: "Pastoral with Pink Horses"; *Anglican Theological Review:* "Was There Evidence of Malpractice?"; *Beloit Poetry Review:* "Seascape with Ghost Crabs and a Nebula"; *The Common:* "A Theory of Pain [We were at a long table . . .]" and "Landscape with Mixed Flowers"; *Gulf Coast:* "The IUD" and "Waiting for Water"; *Indiana Review:* "365 Days" and "21 Weeks [A death not quite]"; *Iowa Review:* "Rupture"; *Juke Joint:* "Domestic Taxonomy [Often, they came with the tide and stayed]"; *Missouri Review:* "After the Baby Dies," "A Theory of Grief [Because dusting is a chore I don't like]," "Authorization for Disposition of Infant Remains," "How to Become Alive Again," and "Sex"; *New Letters:* "Landscape with Tallgrass and Scales" and "Snapshot with Child and Ocean"; *New Ohio Review:* "In Jezero Crater" and "Lightning Dragons"; *Pleiades:* "After the Diagnosis"; *Ploughshares:* "Self-Portrait with IUD Failure"; *RHINO:* "Still Life on the Wrong Side of Statistics" and "21 Weeks [In movies, there are always flowers]"; *Ruminate:* "Snowscape with ADOS-2"; *The Rumpus:* "Mixed Media with Milkweed and an Argument"; *The Rupture:* "Mountainscape with Mule Deer and Cottonwoods"; *South Carolina Review:* "Cityscape Beginning with a Phrase from *Cosmos*" and "Multiverse with Boybands and Roses"; *32 Poems:* "Diagnosis in Reverse"; *Tin House Online:* "Landscape with a Possible Unidentified Flying Object"; *TriQuarterly:* "Landscape with Preterm Labor"; *Waxwing:* "Domestic Taxonomy [Everywhere we went, the animals came]" and "Domestic Taxonomy [The flue was closed, the windows shut]."

"Diagnosis in Reverse" was anthologized in *The Strategic Poet: Honing the Craft* and the *Best American Nonrequired Reading 2019*.

"21 Weeks [In movies, there are always flowers]" won *RHINO*'s 2023 Ralph Hamilton Editors' Prize.

▴ ▴ ▴

I'm grateful for the many people who helped usher this book into being. Thank you to James Long and the whole team at LSU Press, as well as Nancy Reddy for helpful ordering suggestions.

Thank you to my writing professors at UNL—Stacey Waite, Hope Wabuke, Mahtem Shiferraw, and Kwame Dawes—for your help and guidance. Thank you to my poetry cohort at UNL, especially Jess Poli for offering kind words about the book and granting me use of some of those words for marketing material. Thank you to Tara Ballard for those meetings over coffee—I cherished them. I remain awed by the talent and generosity of all the poets and writers I met while at UNL.

Thank you to the poets and writers I met while I lived in Omaha from 2018 to 2024 when I was writing this book, particularly Ted and Nicole Wheeler, Todd

Robinson, Trey Moody, and Carolina Hotchandani. You make Omaha such a vibrant community for writers, and you made me feel like I was part of it.

Thank you to the Vermont Studio Center for supporting this manuscript in its earliest form as I was still trying to dream the first of these poems into being. Thank you to Sandra Lim for choosing my work for the 2022 Maureen Egen Writers Exchange Award, which sent me (and my four-month-old baby) to New York City to meet with writing and publishing professionals. You think you're some sad sack writing elegies in your pajamas, and then you get whisked away on a magical trip where everyone treats you like your writing matters.

Thank you to my parents for their support during some of the events described in this book, particularly for flying across the country twice to take care of Dax when I was hospitalized. Thank you to my mom for going to New York City with me to take care of little River.

Thank you to Niina Pollari for your kindness and for writing *Path of Totality*, a book that met me in my deepest grief. Thank you to Michelle Brunke for being there for me in this terrible club of women who've lost their babies. I'm grateful for you, friend.

Thank you to every kind and understanding teacher and therapist who recognized and appreciated Dax's unique charisma and brilliance and worked hard to guide, teach, and include him. You restore my faith in humanity over and over.

Thank you to Dominic for walking this path with me for over twenty years. All these poems are for you.

www.ingramcontent.com/pod-product-compliance
Lightning Source LLC
Chambersburg PA
CBHW030122170426
43198CB00009B/713